M. J Becker

The Germans of 1849 in America

An Address delivered before the Monday Club of Columbus, Ohio, March 14, 1887

M. J Becker

The Germans of 1849 in America
An Address delivered before the Monday Club of Columbus, Ohio, March 14, 1887

ISBN/EAN: 9783743324756

Manufactured in Europe, USA, Canada, Australia, Japa

Cover: Foto ©ninafisch / pixelio.de

Manufactured and distributed by brebook publishing software
(www.brebook.com)

M. J Becker

The Germans of 1849 in America

THE

Germans of 1849 in America.

AN ADDRESS DELIVERED BEFORE

The Monday Club of Columbus, Ohio,

MARCH 14, 1887.

By M. J. BECKER.

MT. VERNON, O.

THE REPUBLICAN PRINTING HOUSE.

1887.

THE

Germans of 1849 in America.

THIRTY-NINE years ago the Central States of continental Europe were suddenly convulsed by a political commotion, which, although unsuccessful in its immediate objects, has nevertheless left an indelible impression, not only upon the local history of the countries directly concerned, but, indirectly also, upon the affairs of this country, which, in course of time, became the refuge and permanent home of a large number of the prominent actors engaged in that struggle.

For many years prior to 1848 there had been, in various parts of Germany, more or less secret agitation, and a few instances of overt manifestations, indicating the existence of a movement in the direction of political reform. But these demonstrations were not of a well-defined, organized character. The grievances complained of were mostly of local application, and the remedies proposed consequently lacked uniformity of purpose and concentration of effort, and they failed as a matter of course.

But in order to understand the situation and realize the

condition of the country as it existed at the time of which I am about to speak, it will be necessary to sketch, briefly, the preceding history of its people; and since the march of progress in Germany has ever been exceedingly slow, I will be obliged to go back over quite a period of time, so as to trace, in a perceptible measure, the steps of its gradual development.

For nine centuries, prior to its final dissolution in 1806, the various principalities composing the German Empire had been governed, more or less independently, by the princes, dukes, counts, bishops and barons, who, by fair means or foul, by inheritance or conquest, by purchase or exchange, by gambling or by robbery, became possessed of the territories, which, for the time being, they called their own. To follow, even approximately, the constantly-changing outlines of these possessions during the passing centuries, would be well-nigh impossible, even if it were sufficiently interesting, or of importance enough to warrant the hopeless task. As well might we attempt to retain in our memories the varying movements of the ever-shifting clouds in the skies.

In order to maintain themselves against the frequent invasions of foreign foes, and at the same time to control, to a certain extent, the internal relations with each other, these petty rulers had, at an early day, found it necessary to establish some central authority, which, though created by themselves, should be supreme in the exercise of its delegated powers.

The authority thus constituted in the year 911, developed gradually into a system of government, which, under the name of the "Holy Roman Empire," survived, during nine centuries of almost perpetual strife, the numerous wars incident to its own contests for succession, the revolt of the peasants with its attendant atrocities; the thirty years of bloody religious contest in the earlier part of the 17th century; the invasions of the Swedes from the North and the savage raids of the Turks from the South; the incessant dissensions within its own borders and the frequent insurrectionary outbreaks among its own subjects; until, at the end of the last century, it crumbled to pieces under the upheavals of the French Revolution, and finally died in 1806 under the staggering blows dealt by the invincible armies of Napoleon the Great.

The executive head of this central government was chosen by a board of electors, selected from the sovereigns of the separate principalities, partly ecclesiastic and partly secular; and after being crowned by the Pope, the chosen ruler would assume the title of Emperor. Sometimes the crown would descend from father to son and grandson through successive generations; but more frequently the dynastic period would cease with the life of a single ruler, and that life was not always terminated by a death from natural causes.

And during all these years the common people — the serfs and peasants — would toil and starve, that the lords and bishops might feast and carouse.

The soil belonged to the Church, to the barons, and to the lords; and they owned likewise the game in the forest, which the peasant would sometimes be permitted to start up in the chase, not to be slain and eaten by himself, but to be killed at leisure by his lord, and then to be carried by the serf to the kitchen in the castle on the mountain, to be enjoyed by the master and his guests at the banquet in the ancestral hall, after a gay tournament with some knight errant, who, in search of adventure, had come to break a lance for the honor of his lady-love.

This was the age of chivalry and romance, of troubadours and knight-errantry, of which sentimental poets sing in rapture; it was in truth the age of beastly brutality, barbarous ignorance and base superstition: and I am right glad it is over; thanks to Johann Huss, to Philip Melanchthon and Martin Luther, who inaugurated the Great Religious Reformation; to Johann Guttenberg, who invented the printing press : and to Berthold Schwarz, who discovered the explosive property of gunpowder.

The period immediately succeeding the Reformation is especially characterized by the fanatical ferocity of its protracted warfare; the wanton destruction, by fire and sword, of the fertile countries along the Rhine, by the French under Turenne during the reign of Louis XIV., has left in the hearts of the people a deep-seated resentment, which has been nursed through the memories of successive generations, and calls out for vengeance even this day. During the middle of the 18th century, the German Empire was engaged in a long and disastrous war with Frederick the Great, the audacious King of the rapidly-rising new Kingdom of Prussia; and near the end of that century it became involved in a war with the revolutionary leaders of the French Republic, which ended, after the unsuccessful campaign of 1792, in which Prussia had joined the German Emperor, in the temporary peace of 1797; but the renewed aggressions of the restless French Republicans resulted in another war, which again terminated in defeat, followed by another disastrous peace in 1801, by the terms of which the ecclesiastical possessions were abolished, and much territory lost.

Not satisfied yet, the French, upon some trifling pretext, provoked another war in 1805, and once more defeated, not only the German Emperor, but also his allies. England and Russia, in the disastrous battle of Ulm, followed by the overwhelming defeat of Austerlitz, which battle Napoleon, in the pride of his newly-assumed title, delighted to call the battle of the " Three Emperors."

With this defeat ended the German Empire, in the abdication of Francis II. of Austria, in 1806.

The period intervening between the dissolution of the Empire, and the war of deliverance in 1813, embraces the darkest days of Germany's history. Conquered, humiliated, oppressed, insulted; its rulers dethroned, exiled, imprisoned; its male population dragged into the armies of the conqueror, and placed in the front rank of his battles against their own kindred and countrymen; its cities and fortresses garrisoned by the insolent foe, or razed to the ground by treaty stipulations, after successfully resisting siege and assault; the houses of its citizens turned into barracks, the farms devastated and the crops destroyed by the marches, battles and camps of contending armies. These were years of gloom, misery and mourning. But the day of deliverance and retribution came at last.

When Napoleon, with the shivering remnant of his nearly-annihilated army, returned from Russia in the winter of 1812, his involuntary German allies saw their opportunity and deserted him almost to a man. They issued patriotic appeals to their dear subjects to arise, and with "God for King and Country", expel the foreign despot, who, upon the soil of his helpless allies, had been fighting his battles, for the glory of France, with the treasure and blood of his conquered victims. And with these appeals were given fair promises and royal pledges of constitutional liberties and a recognition of the rights of the people. And bravely did the people respond to the royal appeals, and heroically did they rise *en masse*, and never did they stop until the Corsican usurper was safely quartered on board the "Bellerophon," bound for the island beyond the equator where he died; and after the *foreign* despot had been thus disposed of and peace was restored, the good people of Germany, in the first enjoyment of their blessed security and gradually-returning prosperity, did not at once discover that thirty-six *domestic* despots had simply stepped in and quietly taken his place.

When, at last, after the final otherthrow of Napoleon, the victorious princes of Germany repossessed themselves of their principalities, divided the spoils of the conquest, and re-adjusted the boundary lines of their territories, the political and geographical situation was of course very much different from that of the German Empire at the time of its dissolution, ten years before. Prussia had risen, by its own elevation, from a small electorate to a kingdom, as early as 1701, and had maintained its new position through a bloody war of seven years' duration, in spite of the opposition of the German Emperor and nearly all the other powers of Europe combined. Napoleon, after dividing the better portions of Germany between his brother and brother-in-law, had permitted the electors of Bavaria and Wurtemberg to assume the titles of Kings, and rewarded them with an increase of territory for their services and assistance.

The purely ecclesiastical sovereignties had been abolished during the early successes of the French Revolution; the number of free cities had been considerably reduced, and the old landmarks were extensively and radically changed everywhere during the reconstruction of affairs subsequent to the final exportation of Napoleon after his defeat at Waterloo. Yet when, in 1815, they all came together and formed that famous confederation known as the " Bundesrath," there were, exclusive of the free cities, still thirty-six distinct sovereigns left to rule, by the grace of God, over our blessed fatherland.

Twenty years of continuous wars and foreign occupation had thoroughly exhausted the country; and the poor people naturally turned their attention more closely to the restoration of their material interests than to the realization of those dimly-outlined liberties which had been pledged as the reward of their heroic patriotism.

Sweet patience has ever been the German's crowning virtue, and, at the time of which I speak, it was intensified by the re-action which followed an unusual exertion.

The peasants contentedly raised their crops, which were generally small, and uncomplainingly paid their taxes, which were invariably large, realizing, in their stolid way, that their lot was indeed a hard one, but thanking the Lord that it was not worse. The merchants and tradesmen sold their goods for lower prices than they had realized during the inflated period of the war, but they were quite satisfied that they could call the reduced profits their own, and were no longer compelled to pay the ransoms exacted by the marauding Frenchman as an alternative against sacking and pillage.

The so-called " German Bund," or Diet, was an organization composed of the sovereigns of the different states of re-constructed Germany; its fundamental laws were formulated at the Congress of Vienna, after the first deposition of Napoleon, and were afterwards ratified and amplified by the treaty of Paris, after Napoleon's final overthrow. In its original formation, and in its subsequent deliberations and enactments, the people had no voice. Its avowed object was to provide for defence against external enemies, and to guarantee the integrity of the various principalities of which it was composed. It was considered a permanent body, always subject to call after adjournment. Austria held the presiding office; the total number of votes was 71, divided between the 39 states and free cities, each of which had at least one vote — but some of the larger states had four or five. Two-thirds of the votes constituted a majority. A so-called interior or select council, composed of seventeen votes, in which a number of the smaller states collectively represented one vote, and in which simple plurality ruled, was charged with the execution of the measures adopted by the larger body. The meetings were usually held in Frankfurt-on-the-Main, and were generally conducted by accredited ambassadors of the ruling sovereigns, who seldom attended in person.

The original constitution of this " Bund " provided that all the states and principalities composing its organization should establish, within their own territories, constitutional, representative local governments for the administration of their internal affairs; that the exercise of all forms of the Christian religion should be free in all the states, and that the religious status of the Jews should be taken into consideration at an early day; that citizens of one state should be allowed to acquire and own real property in any other state; that, subject to the military duty due by citizens to their native states, emigration and acceptance of civil offices in other states should be permitted. Liberty of the press, in a restricted form, was promised, and rules were established governing copyright; postal regulations, and laws regarding commerce and navigation, were passed; in its relations with the other European powers, the "Bund," representing Germany as a whole, took position as an independent state, sending its own ambassadors to foreign countries, and receiving theirs in return.

Under the provisions of this constitution, a number of the smaller states in Southern Germany had, at an early day, and under various forms, organized constitutional, representative governments; but when, in 1819, some symptoms of political agitation in various parts of the country manifested themselves, the "Bundesrath," in a special session, convened at Karlsbad, so amended its constitution and laws as to materially modify the rights and liberties already granted, and revoking and qualifying many of its pledges for future reforms. At the Congress of Vienna, held by the "Bundesrath" in 1819 and 1820, some further restrictions were placed upon the exercise of previously-granted liberties; commissions were established to supervise the schools and universities; Censors were appointed to regulate all publications, especially the newspaper press and periodicals; and peremptory orders were issued to all the states which had established representative local governments, to the effect that the monarchical principle must be recognized as supreme in all their actions and deliberations.

In 1830, co-incident with the movement in France which sent Charles X. into exile and installed in his place the citizen-king Louis Philippe, Germany became somewhat excited, and loud complaints were uttered everywhere at the long-delayed fulfillment of the promises made in 1815.

In Frankfurt a feeble attempt was made, under the leadership of some university students, to inaugurate an insurrection, which was speedily suppressed, and was followed by imprisonment of the leaders, and by the expulsion of many of the followers. The "Bundesrath" found in this attempt sufficient excuse for further restrictions. All public assemblies, the formation of societies, the wearing of badges, the carrying of flags or banners, were prohibited. Students were forbidden to attend lectures at certain foreign universities: the sale and circulation of a large number of books of certain authors was prohibited under severe penalties, and even the journeymen of the various trades, who from time immemorial had been permitted to pursue their vocations abroad, and who roamed habitually all over the country in search of occupation, were forbidden to visit certain localities, where, it was feared, they might absorb ideas inimical to the interests of monarchical government.

Measures were also taken to perfect the military organization of the "Bund"; the contingent to be furnished by each state for the army was increased; certain fortresses were set apart, and specially garrisoned by the troops of the Federation; and the military relations of the states to the "Bund" and to foreign powers were definitely fixed.

Such, in mere outline, was the condition of Germany prior to the outbreak in the Spring of 1848.

When you consider that the situations and conditions in the different States varied not only among themselves, but lacked uniformity in their relations to the "Bund" as their central authority; that the basis of representation in those states which maintained some semblance of constitutional government rested upon a great variety of conditions; that all these representative bodies depended for their very existence upon the pleasure of the sovereigns who could convene or dissolve them at will; that the governments of the larger states were mere monarchical absolutisms; that the unequal relations which the different states bore to each other gave rise to many difficulties, for which no permanent remedies could be found; that the varying interests of the ruling sovereigns were by no means conducive to harmony among themselves; that the re-division of the different sections of the country, after the establishment of peace, had torn asunder old relations and compelled the amalgamation of new elements which would not readily combine; and when you further add to all this the universal discontent caused by excessive and constantly-increasing taxation, you can imagine that a general feeling of discontent and dissatisfaction prevailed among the people, and that at the very first favorable opportunity they would make demand for such measures of reform, and for redress of such special grievances as each class and occupation would feel to be more particularly oppressive.

This opportunity at last presented itself, when, in the latter part of February, 1848, the stimulus given by the

successful revolution in Paris, which drove Louis Philippe
into exile, aroused the entire continent, and stirred even the
souls of the phlegmatic Germans into action, culminating
during the early Spring in sudden flashes of open revolt in
Berlin, in Vienna and along the Southern borders of the
Duchy of Baden.

Insignificant as these earlier demonstrations must
appear when viewed in the light of subsequent events, they
nevertheless had the effect of wringing from the frightened
rulers partial concessions and promises of future redress.
Relying upon these assurances, the people composed themselves for the moment and quietly devoted the succeeding
summer to the establishment and perfection of such reforma-
tory measures as had been recently inaugurated, the election
of representatives to the state legislatures, and the choosing
of members for the National Parliament which was at last
to lay the foundation for the long-dreamed-of unification of
Germany.

Meantime, the Provisional Government and the ultra-
revolutionary element in France had been overthrown by
the combined re-actionary factions in the sanguinary battles
upon the pavements of Paris in the month of June,
and the popular outbreak in Frankfurt in support of the
measures proposed by the democratic members of Parliament
had been suppressed in September by the cannon and bayonets of the united armies of Prussia, Austria, Hesse and
Bavaria, and, as the winter approached, the emperors, kings
and grand dukes gradually recovered from their fright and
began to breathe easier. The Crown Prince of Prussia (the
present Emperor Wilhelm), who had been chased out of the
the country in March, and had taken refuge in England,
returned to Berlin; the disheartened rulers regained their
courage; a general re-action began; concessions were revoked;
remonstrances were spurned; petitions were haughtily

rejected; riotous demonstrations were put down with unnecessary cruelty and the participants were punished with unusual severity. After the suppression of the rebellion in Vienna, in the autumn of 1848, many of the captives were condemned by court martial and shot.

The winter of 1848 to 1849 was passed in darkest gloom ; the people, discouraged by failure and embittered by disappointment, were growing restless and desperate by degrees.

In the meantime, France, which had given the first impulse, and which had been severely stunned by the staggering blow it had received in June, had now elected, after an exciting campaign, Prince Louis Napoleon as President of the Republic, which meant, as every intelligent observer could even then plainly foresee, a return to a monarchical government.

As a temporary administrator of the affairs of Germany, Parliament had chosen, in the early summer of 1848, the Archduke John of Austria, in whose election the princes of the smaller principalities, and the people generally, aquiesced ; but Austria and Prussia never recognized his authority.

Parliament had also succeeded, after much discussion, in adopting a series of articles embodying the framework for a future constitution. But they failed to give satisfaction to any one : they did not express the wishes of the people, and it was quite apparent that they would not be respected by the rulers.

On the 28th of March, 1849, the imperial crown of Germany was offered by the majority of Parliament to the King of Prussia, Frederick William IV.; the smaller states accepted the choice, but Bavaria, Wurtemberg, Hanover and Saxony refused : Austria formally protested, and after some hesitation, Frederick William himself declined.

Thus were the fruits of a whole year's parliamentary labor lost, and the hopes of the people destroyed. All further efforts by these means appeared now like mockery, and the prolonged deliberations of Parliament henceforth seemed but a farce.

There was but one course left, and that was—Revolution.

It began early in May, 1849, with the expulsion of the Grand Duke of Baden, who, with his family and court, and the higher civil and military officers, departed in great haste at the sudden uprising of his people, who were now fully aroused and in bitter earnest. The rank and file of the army, and a few officers of lower grade, joined the people and established a provisional government at Carlsruhe ; the places of the deserted officers were filled from the ranks and the troops marched to the frontiers to resist the invasion which would be sure to follow, unless equal success should attend simultaneous movements elsewhere. The adjoining Bavarian province across the Rhine followed the example of its neighbors in Baden, and the people took possession of the offices left vacant by the departed functionaries ; the garrisons (excepting that in the Fortress of Landau) fraternized with the people. Volunteers in great numbers poured in from all parts of the country. An uprising had taken place at Dresden, but was suppressed, and the fugitives from Saxony joined the insurgents in Baden and Rhenish Bavaria ; soldiers deserted in many places and swelled the ranks of the Revolutionists, who, for a period of about a month, had things all their own way.

Meantime, Prussia, Hesse-Darmstadt and Nassau gathered up their forces and concentrated them along the Northern borders of Baden and the adjoining states in rebellion ; a few preliminary skirmishes took place on the Southern frontier of Darmstadt, and finally, in the latter part of June, the armies of invasion approached in force along both shores of the Rhine, and also crossed the Bavarian line in two columns from the North and West, converging as they advanced. The Fortress of Landau had remained in possession of the loyal troops of Bavaria, notwithstanding a bold attempt to capture it, and with such a dangerous enemy in the rear, it was not considered safe to risk any decisive engagement in its vicinity : the Revolutionary forces retreated, therefore, slowly before the invading armies, and after a few unimportant engagements, crossed the Rhine opposite Carlsruhe, and joined the better-organized and much larger forces in the Duchy of Baden. A severe engagement was fought at Waghäusel near Mannheim, in which the present Crown Prince of Prussia, who had accompanied his father on this expedition, was slightly wounded, and in which it required the assistance of the Prussian Reserves to maintain the position of the invading army. After another engagement near Upstadt between the Revolutionary troops from Bavaria and the Prussians, the combined forces of the rebellion took position on a line extending from the Rhine on the left to the frontier of Wurtemberg on the right, with the strong Fortress of Rastadt a little to the left of the center. At this point an obstinate resistance was made, and the position was only abandoned after two days of severe fighting, when the troops of the adjoining Kingdom of Wurtemberg crossed the frontier and attacked the insurgents in the rear. With this engagement ended the armed resistance in the field. A large part of the army took shelter in the Fortress of Rastadt, where they withstood a siege of nearly a month, while the remainder, constantly diminished by desertion, retreated slowly before the advancing Prussians and other German troops, through the Black Forest to the borders of Switzerland, where they were disarmed by the Swiss authorities and permitted to take refuge in the different cantons of the confederation. The rank and file were quartered and subsisted at the expense of the Swiss Government, until they gradually took advantage of the proffered pardon and returned home. The leaders, who could not return, settled down temporarily in various parts of Switzerland; but in the Spring of 1850 the Swiss Government, under pressure from its surrounding neighbors, induced, under the promise of assistance, the greater number to leave the country. A general exodus followed; Holland, Belgium, South America and England were sought by many, but by far the greater number embarked for the United States at once.

The struggles, hardships, privations and sufferings endured by most of these men during the earlier days of their American experience would form extremely interesting, but in many instances very sad chapters in the histories of their checkered lives. Many fell by the wayside exhausted, and died of want in the crowded cities of the Eastern coast; some, in utter despair, cut short, with their own hands, the hopeless misery of their wretched existence. That the occupations which some were forced to accept did not in all cases afford opportunities for improving the advantages of their earlier education, may be readily imagined. I remember well, that in my own case, while I was trimming toothsome bunches of bright red early radishes, and tying up bundles of fragrant young onions for the daily market, long before the rising of the summer sun, upon a garden farm on Long Island, I often bewailed the misdirected applications of my early youth; and even the mathematical tracing of the parallel furrows for the transplanting of beets and cabbages, and the engineering precision displayed in the setting out of the succulent tomato vines, failed to satisfy my professional ambition; nor did I consider the compensation of four dollars per month for fifteen hours of daily toil an adequate reward for skilled labor like this. It is true, I had board and lodging besides. The board, I am bound to say, was inferior in kind, though ample in quantity; but the lodging was on a most liberal scale. I had the whole of Long Island to sleep on, with millions of mosquitoes sweetly singing their lullabys.

One day I met, in the lower part of New York, a young sculptor, who in his early youth had been a school-fellow of mine, and who, while pursuing his studies at the Academy of Fine Arts in Paris, had been drawn into the common whirlpool of rebellion, and after drifting about for a while in Belgium and England, had arrived in America a short time before. Although still quite young, he had achieved remarkable success, and had been rewarded with a prize medal in recognition of his talent and genius. We were glad to see each other. After a rapid exchange of experiences, I ventured to ask how he was prospering in his profession. "Ah, you should come to my studio and see for yourself," he said ; "I am just now engaged in putting the last finishing touches upon some magnificent masterpieces of plastic art ; you must see them, before they leave my studio." Responding to his invitation, I found him, a few days afterwards, in a low, dingy back room of a small carpenter shop in Greenwich Street, busily engaged in rubbing down with sandpaper the colossal limbs of a wooden Pocohontas, destined to adorn the entrance door of a tobacco shop.

But in accordance with the law of natural selection, in the universal struggle for existence, the fittest will always survive; and if I have not already completely exhausted your patience, I will sketch, in brief outlines, the histories of a few of the prominent survivors of this struggle.

FREDERICK HECKER.

First in point of time, and foremost in prominence and distinction, came Frederick Hecker.

When, after the few temporary popular successes of the early Spring of 1848, the people throughout Germany, elated with their triumphs, confiding in the promises of their vanquished and compliant rulers, and hoping for a peaceful realization of their long-cherished hopes, sent their hastily-chosen representatives to the Provisional Convention at Frankfurt, with instructions to formulate the outlines and construct the rudimentary framework upon which the eventual permanent Parliament should build its ship of state, Hecker, who had been chosen as one of the delegates, realized, at an early day, that it would be in vain to look to this body for the realization of his hopes. There was manifestly a very wide division among the delegates regarding the general objects in view; and while they all agreed that the spirit of the age demanded some measures of reform, it soon became evident, that in regard to their range and extent, and the means of accomplishing them, the sentiment of the Convention was greatly divided. The conservative side of the house insisted upon the fullest maintenance of the prerogatives of the ruling sovereigns, and the strictest adherence to the monarchical form of government; and they limited their concessions to the people to a restricted system of representation, a moderate exercise of the liberty of the press under governmental supervision, and the right to assemble for peaceable purposes by special permission; they preferred the continuance of the old " Bundesrath " — with some modifications — as the central government for united Germany.

The moderate liberal party of progression demanded

constitutional monarchical governments, with responsible cabinet ministers for the several states; unrestricted liberty of the press; a reduction of the standing armies, and an Emperor for the ruler of united Germany, to be elected by Parliament. The radical members of the extreme left called aloud for immediate abdication of the ruling sovereigns, total abolishment of the standing armies, and a republican government for all Germany, including Schleswig and Holstein, the German-speaking provinces of Denmark.

Between these three leading factions there were many intermediate shades of political creeds, but the extremest member of the extreme republican left was Frederick Hecker. There was no question regarding his platform, and there was no such word as "compromise" in his political vocabulary. He soon turned his back upon the Convention, and, in a passionate, eloquent appeal, called his constituents of the Lake District from the North shore of Constance, to arms. And heartily did they respond with such arms as they had. With guns of every pattern from the days of the arquebuse down, with swords dating back to the crusades, they came; pikes and lances they bore; battle-axes and pistols of ancient make; but by far the greater number bore the weapon of old Saturn himself, scythes fastened straight to their handles, with blades sharpened and whetted to the keenness of a razor's edge. Formidable weapons they were, indeed, for close range, but of very little avail against the needle guns of the army; and when, after a short parley upon the field near Kanderen, the troops sent a volley of minie-balls rattling through the scythe-blades, the insurgents fled and dispersed, and the armed rebellion collapsed. This was in May, 1848.

Hecker, mortified and sorely disappointed, took refuge

in America, and settled, with a few of his immediate friends, near Belleville, in Illinois.

He had been the leader and parliamentary champion of the people in that first crude and primitive specimen of representative government in Germany, the Chamber of Deputies of the Grand Duchy of Baden, for a number of years prior to 1848. Eloquent, sincere, enthusiastically devoted to the people by whom he had been chosen, he enjoyed, in return, a popularity seldom attained by mortal man. Of handsome presence, graceful figure and impressive countenance, frank in speech, prompt in action, he was idolized by men and women alike. The famous Hecker Song could be heard upon the highways and byways of Southern Germany, in village and city, sung early and late, by young and by old, with enthusiastic fervor, and *encored* to the echo.

Of sanguine temperament himself, personally brave and fearless to a fault, it is not surprising that he, flattered by every possible manifestation of popular devotion, and believing firmly in the righteousness of his cause, did not only count upon the fullest support of his own people, but confidently expected to win over to his side the very soldiers who were sent to destroy him. How deep must have been his grief, how sore his mortification, at the sad failure of his effort. Still, when in the following Spring the news of the second uprising in his native country reached him in his Western home, he hastened, with all the enthusiasm of his fervent nature rekindled, across the ocean, only to learn, upon landing, the far more disastrous failure and the far more bloody defeat of the cause for whose success he would have gladly given his life.

Sorrowful and almost heart-broken, he returned to his American home, leading for many years the quiet life of a Western farmer, visited occasionally by old friends, exiled from their country like himself, pursuing, in his modest way, the laborious duties of his new occupation, respected for his sterling worth, beloved for his honesty and integrity, and admired by all who knew him, for the grand yet simple traits of his character.

When our own rebellion shook the Union from centre to circumference, Frederick Hecker hastened to the defence of his adopted country with a full regiment of men, enlisted by himself. The 82d Illinois, or so-called Hecker regiment, composed principally of German soldiers, did credit to itself and to its commander throughout the war, from which he returned at its close, with a severe wound, sorely crippled for life.

The honest sincerity and enthusiastic fervor with which he performed his duties, and which frequently assumed a degree of energy bordering on vehemence, led him occasionally into ludicrous and embarassing situations.

At the re-election of Abraham Lincoln in the fall of 1864, Hecker ordered his regiment out in full dress, armed and equipped, and marched the men to the polls with bayonets fixed, drums beating and colors flying; and the soldiers voted for old Abe to a man. When Mr. Lincoln, who had known Hecker well as a neighbor in Illinois, heard of this he felt greatly annoyed, and sent for him, and remonstrated with him for committing such a flagrant breach of propriety. Hecker quite seriously and earnestly contended that there was nothing wrong in his conduct; if it was proper to vote at all, it could not be improper to do it in good style; and, as a justifying precedent, he told Mr. Lincoln that in the days of ancient Rome the legions always emphasized their suffrage by striking their brazen shields with their swords. But honest old Abe did not seem to appreciate the application and failed to see the similarity between a regiment of Suckers from Western

Illinois and a Roman legion; nor would he admit the semblance between himself and an Imperial Cæsar.

~ After Hecker's return from his four years' service in the army, he found that the quiet life on the farm did no longer agree with him; his crippled condition interfered with his occupation; and the idle hours dragged heavily. For a season he sought relief and diversion in a lecturing tour, but met with indifferent success; the subjects chosen for his discourses, although treated with consummate, scholarly skill, were not adapted for his audiences; his place was the tribune, not the platform.

Shortly after the Franco-German war Hecker made a visit to his old home in Germany, where he was enthusiastically received by his former friends and neighbors, with whom he rejoiced heartily over the final realization of his hopes, the recently-accomplished unification of Germany.

After his return to America he gradually retired from active life; the infirmities of old age, attended sometimes with intense suffering, crept on apace, and he died five years ago at his country home near Belleville, honored by all who ever knew him, for his uncompromising honesty and sterling integrity.

CARL SCHURZ.

The man, who, on account of his superior education, and by virtue of his unquestioned talent and great natural ability, could and should have become the foremost representative German in America, is Carl Schurz. But the attainment of such distinction could never have been his ambition; for the success which has always attended his efforts in other directions, would certainly have been a sufficient guarantee for ample reward in this, if he had seen proper to make the attempt. Perhaps he felt, that by giving his services to the

whole country of his adoption, he would, at the same
time, best promote the special interests of his native countrymen. However that may have been, it is quite certain, that
while he acquired fame, he lost popularity, and while he
gained distinction, he sacrificed the affection of his people.
And yet, no one ever suspected the honesty of his motives
or questioned the sincerity of his intentions; but he lacks
that straightforward, open-hearted, cheerful adherence to a
correct principle and the steadfast support of a righteous
cause, which pardons minor faults and generously overlooks
trifling defects: he is deficient in that charity which is will-
ing to spare the doomed city, if there can be found but
three righteous people within its walls; still, I am inclined
to ascribe to an ill-conceived sense of duty these failings,
which others have attributed to cold-hearted, mercenary
selfishness. Indeed, it would be impossible for a cold-
hearted, selfish character to possess the self-sacrificing devotion which Schurz displayed, when, after having safely
escaped capture, he bravely risked his own life in the
rescue of his imprisoned friend, Gottfried Kinkel, under
difficulties which called forth the exercise of the highest
courage and the most heroic perseverance.

At the commencement of the revolutionary movement
in 1848, Schurz was a student at the University of Bonn,
where his friend, Professor Kinkel, was reading lectures on
literature. The out-break in 1849 brought both to the seat
of war, where Kinkel enlisted in Willich's Corps of Volunteers, and fell during the battle at Rastadt, dangerously
wounded, into the hands of the Prussians. Schurz served
as aid to Frederick Anneke, who had assumed command
of the artillery in the fortress. After the retreat of the
army from the field around Rastadt, the fortress was
invested and beseiged, and finally capitulated. But during
the night preceding the final surrender, Schurz made his

escape through sewers and ditches and crossed the Rhine in safety. Kinkel, who was a Prussian subject and soldier, and who had been captured while fighting against the army of his sovereign, was sentenced to be shot, and would have been executed, if he had not been rescued by Schurz's daring effort. They finally landed in England, where Kinkel remained; but Schurz soon came to America and settled at Watertown, in Wisconsin. His general ability, especially his eloquence, soon brought him into prominence, and as early as 1856 he carried by storm such far-famed masters of oratory as Sumner and Wendell Philips by a speech which he made at a banquet in Boston. In 1860 he was a delegate to the National Convention which nominated Lincoln, whom he ardently supported during that memorable canvass which resulted in his election. After the inauguration, Schurz was appointed Minister to Spain, which office he soon resigned to take a command in the army. His military service, although not distinguished for any particularly remarkable achievements, has been uniformly honorable and creditable. It is admitted by those who knew him then, and had opportunities to judge, that he was a brave, devoted soldier, dutiful and sincere. His military record is voluminous, and the range of his activity quite extensive. In August, 1862, he commanded the 3d Division of Sigel's 1st Corps during Pope's campaign at Manassas. In May, 1863, he fought at Chancellorsville at the head of a division in the 11th Corps; in July of the same year he was at Gettysburgh, where he assumed temporary command of the entire 11th Corps, when Gen. Howard, after Reynold's death, was placed in charge of the 1st, 3d and 11th Corps combined; on the first day of that battle Schurz displayed great personal courage in attempting to rally the routed troops of his Corps, and on the second day he repulsed a fierce attack of the rebels upon Cemetery Hill, where his headquarters were.

Transferred with Gen. Hooker to the West, he fought before Chattanooga in September, and in November took part in the storming of Missionary Ridge.

After the close of the war he was sent by President Johnson, together with Generals Grant and Thomas, upon a commission of inspection into the Southern States, to report upon their condition and ascertain the sentiments of the people. During his term in the United States Senate he gave offence to the ultra Republicans by his open advocacy of a conciliatory policy towards the South; his speeches on the St. Domingo Treaty and on the German Arms question were masterpieces of brilliant oratory and logical argument. The clear, concise and comprehensive manner with which he treated the financial question during the inflation heresy of a few years ago, is admitted by all fair-minded people to be convincing, exhaustive and unanswerable. As a Cabinet Minister during the uneventful administration of President Hayes, he conducted the affairs of his Department on plain but strict business principles, and left the public service with the undisputed reputation of being an honest man. His subsequent career upon the field of political journalism has been characterized by a hypercritical treatment of the living issues of the day, and by the assumption of negative positions between the parties, which satisfied neither, and simply made it necessary for himself to desert to the enemy in order to punish his friends; and having repeated this operation rather too often, he is now left alone in the hands of his enemies, with no friends left to be punished.

ALEXANDER SCHIMMELPFENNIG.

The secret agitations which for a number of years preceded the final outbreak in 1848, extended, in some few instances, among the officers of the Prussian army. The principal centers of this movement were in Westphalia and among the garrisons along the lower Rhine; the officers of the artillery regiments stationed in Cologne, Wesel, Munster and Minden were especially affected. Some of the officers of the infantry also caught the contagion. As the movement spread, it became more and more difficult to maintain secresy; discoveries were made by spies and detectives, followed by peremptory dismissals of some, and the forced resignation of others. The 7th Regiment of Artillery was almost dismembered by dismissals of its officers during the years of 1846 and 1847. Among them were August Willich, Joseph Weidemeyer and Frederick Anneke.

Among the infantry officers who left the service about that time was Alexander Schimmelpfennig. He had been a Lieutenant in the 29th Regiment of Infantry, stationed in my native city of Coblentz, and when I met him in May, 1849, at Ludwigshafen, opposite Mannheim, just after Col. Blenker had captured the Bavarian end of the pontoon bridge over the Rhine at that point, we naturally became acquainted and mutually attached to each other. He was then quite young, short and lithe of stature, blonde and fair, aggressive, combative, a little haughty, but genial, and quite dashing, the very picture and ideal of the typical sub-lieutenant of the Prussian army. His silky, cream-colored mustache was curled up defiantly at both ends, and he carried his dimpled chin high up in the air like a boy with a chip on his shoulder. After a few days he was assigned by the Provisional Government of Trans-Rhenish Bavaria to the command of some of the regular troops who had gone over to our side, and of the volunteers who were flocking in from all parts of the country, and which he stationed along the Prussian frontier, with headquarters at Zweibrucken. Upon my arrival at this town soon afterwards, I was detailed for service as aid to the Civil Commissary of the District, Doctor Weiss, now a resident of Buffalo, N. Y., to whose fatherly care and friendly interest I am indebted for my existence to-day. While Schimmelpfennig drilled his recruits, I assisted Doctor Weiss in collecting the revenue from the adjacent coal mines and salt works, by a process so expeditious and prompt that it could properly be classed under the head of " direct taxation." This lasted for about three weeks, but one fine morning two Prussian columns marched over the border, under the command of the Crown Prince of Prussia, scattered Schimmelpfennig's regulars and volunteers, and while he was trying to check the rout, a Prussian rifle-ball pierced his leg. On that same morning, before I went out on my last revenue errand, I had borrowed a pair of boots from Schimmelpfennig, to wear while my own were undergoing repair. When I met Schimmelpfennig in the afternoon, on the retreat between Zweibrucken and Landau, stretched out in an ambulance, he laughingly said, " Keep the boots, my boy, I will not need them for a while." Three or four months later, after we had passed over the border into Switzerland, I met him again in Zurich and returned his boots, somewhat the worse for wear during the preceding campaign and retreat.

I never saw him again, nor even heard of him, until his name was mentioned in the newspapers as a possible colonel for a regiment of Germans, enlisted for the war in the Spring of 1861.

He served under Sigel in the Army of the Potomac

during the campaign of Gen. Pope, fought bravely at Groveton, and was promoted for gallantry at the second battle of Bull Run. At Chancellorsville he commanded the first brigade of Schurz's Division of the 11th Corps. At Gettysburgh he commanded Schurz's Division on the first day, and fought with distinction upon Cemetery Ridge on the second day of that battle. In February, 1864, he was sent to St. John's Island in Charleston Harbor, and in February, 1865, he entered that rebellious city at the head of his Division, the first Union soldier to set foot upon its streets since the firing on Sumter.

His health had become seriously impaired during the the last year of the war, and he died from the effects of his exposures in the swamps of South Carolina, in September, 1865, at Minersville, Pa.

FREDERICK KAPP.

But the brightest, most genial and truly lovable character of all was Frederick Kapp. He was born in the town of Hamm, in the Prussian Province of Westphalia, where his father was Principal of the Gymnasium, as the German colleges are called. Whoever has traveled through that part of Germany, must have been attracted by the singular beauty and physical perfection of its people. Tall of stature, muscular and erect in carriage, with rosy cheeks and fair complexions, clear blue eyes and curling hair of golden hue, the very peasants are models of statuesque beauty and grace; and of this type, Kapp was a superior specimen.

Full of health and manly strength, his kindly eyes fairly aglow with merriment and good humor, he delighted to tell his jolly stories and deliver his witty sallies in that peculiar lisping Westphalian accent, which to a Southern

German has always a peculiar charm. His features were clear-cut, regular, and expressive of strength and character, but his good-natured smile secured him at first sight the lasting friendship of all; nor did the deep-cut scar on his right cheek, a relic of his Heidelberg University days, mar in the least his handsome face.

Completing at an early age his college studies under the immediate tuition of his excellent father, he studied jurisprudence first at Heidelberg and then at Berlin, where he also served his military time as volunteer in the Artillery of the Guard. He had just been assigned to duty as a young advocate at the Superior Court in his native town of Hamm when the Revolution of 1848 broke out in Paris and spread over Germany with lightning speed. After taking an active part in the agitation preceding the elections, he took up his residence in Frankfurt at the assembling of Parliament in that city, where he remained as correspondent for some of the leading journals of the day, until the bloody insurrection in September, during which Count Lychnovski and Baron von Auerswald, reactionary members of Parliament, were killed, when he found it prudent to remove to Paris, which was just then beginning to be agitated by the movement which resulted in the election of Louis Napoleon as President in the following December.

During the winter of 1848 and 1849, Kapp remained in Paris, engaged as correspondent for various journals and contributor to several German periodicals.

In May and June, 1849, while we were in the field against the Prussians, in Southern Germany, Kapp came over once or twice to visit us; but he did not take any active part in that campaign; and when, after its disastrous conclusion, we retreated into Switzerland, I found him, in August, at Geneva, living in the family of the famous

Russian revolutionist, Alexander Herzen, whose literary
works he prepared for publication, while, at the same time,
he was entrusted with the education of Herzen's young
son. Early in 1850 he came to New York, where he first
engaged in literary work, publishing among other works a
clear and concise history of slavery in the United States,
which little volume contributed largely to the enlighten-
ment of the German population on this important topic,
which just then occupied such a large share in the political
affairs of this country. He became also editor of a newspaper called the *Evening Gazette*, published by a co-opera-
tive association of printers. He wrote the lives of Baron
Steuben and of de Kalb, both of which were translated
into English, and obtained quite an extensive circulation.
Later, when he had been appointed Commissioner of
Emigration, he wrote a general history of emigration, which
contains much interesting statistical information. During
nearly all this time he conducted, in partnership with Zitz
and Froebel, a foreign exchange business. Both these part-
ners had been prominent in the political affairs of Germany;
both had been members of Parliament; Zitz represented the
city of Mainz. Froebel, who was a brother of the founder
of the now well-known Kindergarten method for the early
education of children, had taken an active part in the revolutionary movement in Vienna during the summer of 1848.
When that city was finally retaken by the troops of the
Emperor of Austria, who had been compelled, at the
outbreak, to flee for his life and hide himself at Insbruck in
the Tyrol, Froebel was captured, together with Robert
Blum, another member of Parliament, from the city of
Cologne, and both were condemned by court martial to be
shot. Blum was executed, but Froebel was pardoned,
quite unexpectedly, at the very last moment, and released
unconditionally.

The firm of Zitz, Kapp & Froebel dissolved sometime during the sixties, and Kapp returned to his native country about the time of the Franco-German war, and was soon afterward elected to the Imperial Parliament, in which he served with credit to himself, and to the recognized satisfaction of his constituents, until the time of his death about two years ago.

CHRISTIAN ESSELLEN.

Among the early school-fellows and subsequent college mates and university chums of Frederick Kapp was Christian Essellen, whose career I will briefly mention by way of contrast.

His father was a quiet, unobtrusive, respectable old gentlemen, an official of the Superior Court in the town of Hamm, in Westphalia, with a small salary, but with a very formidable title, long enough, as his wicked son mockingly delighted to tell us, to constitute a complete hexameter by itself. Listen, and hear how it sounds: "Oberlandesgerichtssalariencassenrendant." Nineteen syllables and thirty-nine letters in one word; fourteen vowels and twenty-five consonants. And what do you suppose it all means? Listen, again, and I will tell you. It means that the poor old man was the cashier of a treasury in which were deposited the funds for the payment of the salaries of the officers of the Superior Court. Who will dare tell me after this that my native tongue is not concise and expressive? Out of his small income the poor old gentleman with the extensive title managed to give his son Christian a first-class education, which, assisted by a phenomenally bright intellect, developed, at an unusually early age, a mind of rarest brilliancy. Before he was nineteen he wrote a tragedy, "Rienzi Cola," the superior merit of which was acknowl-

edged at the time by critical judges in most flattering terms.
But with the acquisition of knowledge he absorbed the
poison of evil. He left the university an intellectual giant,
but at the same time a moral wreck. He became a slave to
every vice; he made no attempt to resist temptation, but
appeared to take a fiendish delight in offending every virtue
and defying every law. He was the very incarnation of a
reckless rebel against every rule of decency and the
common code of propriety; but through all his amazing
wickedness shone the brilliant light of his genius. Socially
he could be the most delightful companion, bright, witty
and sparkling, but in a moment he would turn into an
offensive, unmitigated nuisance.

The year of his military service in Berlin he spent
chiefly under arrest, and upon his discharge from the army
he plunged at once into the turbulent political agitation
which just then was at its fever height. In times like
those, the extremest leader always commands the largest
following. Reckless in manner, bold and defiant in utter-
ance, attractive withal in his youthful daring, he was the
idol of the rabble and the favorite of the masses. He would
himself go as far as any one dared to follow. The Rebellion of 1849 found him, of course, at the center of its
greatest commotion. He had studied law at the Universities of Berlin and Heidelberg, and on the strength of this
accomplishment, in mockery of the blind-folded goddess, he
served in the capacity of Judge Advocate to the Provisional
Government at Carlsruhe, during the brief period of its
existence.

Driven with the rest over the borders into Switzerland,
left without occupation or employment, he passed through
a course of wildest dissipations, which only ceased with his
physical exhaustion. Reduced to a mere shadow of his
former self, with trembling nerves and twitching muscles,

he crossed the Channel into England, and, after a short residence there, during which he seemed to have partly recovered himself, he came to this country in 1852 or 1853. Here he made his last honest effort at reformation, and for a time there was some hope of success. During this period he became associated, in Cleveland, with your former townsman, J. H. Klippart, whom, no doubt, many of you will remember as the able and efficient Secretary of the State Board of Agriculture, whose many valuable contributions to the literature of his department have greatly promoted the material development of the agricultural interests of this state.

Together, Essellen and Klippart published, somewhere in 1855 or 1856, a periodical under the name of *American Liberal*. It was ably edited, but its career was short.

After the cessation of this periodical, Essellen returned to the East to relapse into dissipation and to die. His last days were spent in an asylum for inebriates upon Blackwell's Island; and after he had breathed his last, and was resting in his coffin, while some of his old friends were standing mournfully by his side, another inmate of the same institution, likewise a participant in the rebellion and now an exile, Count Fenner von Fenneberg, an Austrian nobleman, and once a distinguished officer in the German army, while laboring under a fit of insanity, burst into the room of the dead, and insisted upon delivering a funeral oration over the body of his departed friend.

With this ghastly scene closed the history of Christian Essellen's wretched life.

FRANZ SIGEL

was one of the few officers of the regular army of the Duchy of Baden, who did not follow their Grand Duke into exile at the outbreak in 1849, but tendered their services to the revolutionary government. Sigel was offered the commandership of all the forces, but he modestly declined the acceptance of such responsibility, feeling, no doubt, a want of confidence in his ability, owing to his lack of experience. But when the last engagement had been fought, and the two Polish commanders, Generals Sznyda and Mieroslawski, had failed to realize the success which had been expected under their leadership, the soldiers clamored for Sigel, who thereupon assumed command of the army and conducted the final retreat into Switzerland. During his exile in Geneva and Zurich, Sigel led a very retired life, keeping aloof from his comrades and avoiding all social intercourse. Little was known of him then, and, aside from his military record, little is known of him now. If he is a great man, he has failed to show it, although his opportunities have been ample. As a soldier he displayed skill and achieved some success while in subordinate commands, but when placed in positions of greater responsibility he did not succeed in taking the advantage of his opportunities which a more ambitious man would have secured by promptness of action and decision of character. Wherever he displayed any ability it was in secondary affairs and minor details. His famous retreat from Carthage in Missouri, in July, 1861, before Governor Jackson's superior forces, was simply a skillfully-executed artillery maneuver, and this was the arm of the service in which Sigel had been especially trained. At Wilson's Creek and Pea Ridge his professional acquirements again came in good play on a limited scale, and brought his name into such prominence, that, when the Army of Virginia was organized in June, 1862, under Pope, Sigel was assigned to the command of the 1st Corps, after Fremont, who was unwilling to serve under Pope, had resigned. Between

Pope and Sigel frequent misunderstandings arose regarding the meaning of orders on the one side, and their interpretation and execution on the other, which led to ill-natured reproaches on the part of Pope, and surly responses and peevish action on the part of Sigel. These quarrels continued through the operations in the Shenandoah Valley, and culminated in criminating charges against Sigel after the second battle of Bull Run. But this battle also ended Pope's career, who was relieved by McClellan just prior to the Antietam campaign, during which Sigel commanded the 11th Corps of the re-organized army. When Hooker succeeded McClellan he relieved Sigel from command just as the army started for Chancellorsville, and, as there appeared to be no special reason for this seeming degradation, it may be true that the bad behavior of the soldiers of the 11th Corps in that engagement, at least partly, was due to their demoralization on account of the ill-treatment of their commander.

With this retirement from command ended Sigel's active share in the war. Since that time he has lived in comparative seclusion in New York. Once or twice he has taken part in political campaigns, speaking to the Germans, and defending, if I remember right, the Democratic side of the issue. He has held various offices in the city and state, and is now serving the Government of the United States as Pension Agent for the district of New York City. He is known, and will be remembered, for the prominent positions he occupied rather than for the deeds he accomplished.

AUGUST WILLICH.

Among the Prussian officers who were dismissed in 1847, on account of their participation in political movements, was Captain August Willich, of the 7th Regiment of Artillery. He was of noble birth, and the descendant of a long line of soldiers distinguished for bravery in the military service of their country, and he was, every inch of him, a magnificent soldier himself. In the Spring of 1848 he joined the forces under Hecker in Baden, and, after a short exile in France, he returned in September with Gustave Struve for a second attempt, and after the failure of that invasion, he retired with a number of his men to the town of Besancon, on the Western slope of the Jura Mountains, which here form the boundary between Switzerland and France. Here he organized his fellow exiles into a military company, and drilled them as only he could drill. When the general uprising took place in May, 1849, Willich reported promptly for duty with his body of refugees, veterans in rebellion, and took a prominent part in the two days' engagement at Rastadt. After the retreat of the army into Switzerland, Willich again retired to Besancon, but was soon compelled by the French Government to leave; whereupon he embarked for England some time in 1850, and after a year or two came to America, where he found employment in one of the engineering parties of the Coast Survey. Subsequently he came to Cincinnati, and engaged in journalism. At the outbreak of our own Civil War, Willich enlisted at once in Robert McCook's 9th Ohio Regiment, which was largely composed of soldiers trained in the armies of Germany. He was appointed Adjutant, and when that regiment left Camp Dennison for the seat of war in West Virginia, there was not its equal, among the volunteer forces in the service, for general efficiency. While engaged in the West Virginia campaign, Willich attracted the attention of Governor Morton, of Indiana, who offered him the Colonelcy of the 32d Regiment of Infantry from that State, which he accepted, and in command of which he remained until promoted to a higher rank.

It is no exaggeration to say, that, as a soldier, Willich was perfection itself, and it is no disparagement, for it is but the simple truth, to add, that he was absolutely unfit for anything else. It was inspiring to see him draw his sword, and it was positively humiliating to see his awkward attempts at the performance of the simplest duties of ordinary life. He fought at Perryville under Alexander McCook; at Stone River he was captured, in consequence of his anxiety to report personally to his chief the movements of some rebel troops on his flank, which led him to ride to headquarters alone, and running straight into the enemy's lines on his return. At Mumfordville, the superior training of his regiment enabled it to resist, though scattered out in skirmish line, a sudden and very fierce attack of a regiment of Texas Rangers, killing its Colonel and repulsing the troopers with heavy loss. This little fight is described as one of the most brilliant achievements of the war. A little yellow, white-maned Texas mustang, which was captured by Willich on that occasion, was sent by the captor to the young son of Judge Stallo, at Mount Auburn, where it became the pet of the neighborhood.

Willich arrived at Shiloh in command of the 32d Indiana early on Monday morning, and at once made a gallant attack on the enemy, but met with stubborn resistance. Finding that under the heavy fire some of his men began to lose self-control, he stepped in front, and for fully ten minutes drilled them in the manual of arms, as he said, to cool them off, and make them steady, and then continued the fight.

It is sufficient to say, that at Chickamauga he was with Thomas. In one of the engagements near Atlanta he received a severe wound in his upper right arm, which disabled him for active service, and, upon his partial recovery, he was placed in command of the post of Cincinnati, where he remained until the close of the war.

The old saying, that Republics are ungrateful, is, like many other old sayings, only partly true; but the manner in which they manifest their gratitude leaves it sometimes questionable whether the reward is not a punishment. When a good man has served his country well in one capacity, he is generally made to serve it in another for which he is wholly unfit. The election of General Willich as Auditor of Hamilton County is a flagrant example of this kind, intensified by a repetition. It was the intention to give the brave old soldier an opportunity to save, out of the large income of his office, enough to make himself comfortable for the rest of his days; but he had no more idea of saving money for himself than he had of auditing the accounts of his office. He became the easy victim of insinuating imposters, and the favorite subject of visionary cranks; and though he paid dearly for his experiences, he did not profit by their lessons. To save him at last from actual want in his old age, his friends secured, during the last year of his second term, a part of his income, and invested it in such a manner that he could not dispose of it, except in small amounts gradually drawn out. Depending upon these allowances for his subsistence, and being of frugal habits, he managed to live abroad for several years, attending lectures on philosophy at the University in the same city of Berlin where, nearly fifty years before, he had studied the science of war as a youthful cadet. Upon his return to this country he settled in the quiet little village of Saint Marys, in Auglaize County, near some old friends of his soldier days, and pursued, with the enthusiasm of a school-boy, the studies he had commenced at the Berlin

University, spending his leisure in frolicsome plays with the children of the village, whose dearest friend he was.

One night he retired in good health and spirits, and the next morning he was missed by the children at the playground. He had died during the night, apparently without a struggle.

FREDERICK ANNEKE.

Among the officers of the Westphalian Artillery Regiment who left the service prior to the outbreak in 1848, was Frederick Anneke. He was a First Lieutenant at the time of his discharge. He was quiet, studious, reticent, almost morose, but positive in his convictions and determined in his actions. He took a prominent part in the movements of the Spring of 1848 in Munster and in Cologne, where for a time he was imprisoned, with others, for making inflammatory speeches and for issuing incendiary publications. In May, 1849, he was made Chief of Artillery of the revolutionary army in Baden, and as such took command of the artillery in the Fortress of Rastadt; but, knowing well that in case of his capture at the eventual surrender he would certainly be shot, he made his escape from the Fortress just before its investment, and retired with the army into Switzerland. After a short residence in England, he came to the United States, and settled in Milwaukee. If he took any part in our own war of Rebellion, it could not have been a very conspicuous one, but I think he was absent in Europe at that time on account of ill health. He died in Chicago about ten years ago. His wife, Mathilda Francisca Anneke, survived him until two years ago. She was a woman of distinguished character and rare accomplishments. In her youth she was quite famous for her beauty and dignified grace; she had been married at an early age to a Westphalian nobleman of dissipated habits and brutal instincts, who ill-treated her until she was compelled to leave him and obtain a divorce. She married Anneke a short time after his discharge from the army. Prior to this she had written several books of local history, and also some works of fiction. She accompanied her husband during the entire campaign of 1849, and shared his subsequent exile.

In Milwaukee she established a school for the education of young ladies, which appears to have been well conducted, and largely patronized by the best people of the city and neighborhood. Her voice was very sweet and melodious : her language always earnest, dignified and impressive; the subjects of her discourse were always chosen with taste, tact and sound judgment, while her manners were graceful and pleasing.

The life work of such a woman cannot be wasted, and we can safely take it for granted that the beneficial influence of her teachings and example will be felt, and gratefully appreciated, by her pupils and their descendants, for generations yet to come.

CARL HEINZEN

was a distinguished journalist and an accomplished writer of wonderful force and influence; concise and clear in his statements, logical and convincing in his arguments, bitter and fierce in his denunciations, and relentless in his persecution; a severe, uncompromising critic; a man to be admired, but feared rather than loved.

His prolific pen had kept the German censors busy for many years prior to the Revolution. Most of his publication were confiscated, on general principles, as soon as they left the press, unless they had already been seized by the police in the composing room.

Physically, he was a man of gigantic frame, six feet or more in height, able-bodied and strong; but there was no fight in him. He seemed to feel that his pen was mightier than his sword, and he preferred to attack the enemy at long range with fierce pronunciamentos and soul-stirring harangues; but never a drop of blood would he spill— neither the enemy's nor his own; and while the rest of us fought and then ran away so as to live and fight some other day. Heinzen, who had never fought at all, ran away with the others, but evidently more with a view of saving his life for the time being than with the intention of renewing the fight at some future day.

During our refuge in Geneva, we lived close together at Grand Pré, on the hedge-lined road to Petit-Sacconnex, near the country-seat of Albert Galère, whose hospitable house was made the cheerful home for many a wanderer during the dreary winter of 1849. At a little cabaret, where the red wine from Tessin and the purple-tinted mélange from Canton de Vaux 'were sold so cheap that even we, the poverty-stricken members of the so-called "Brimstone Club," could afford to drink them on credit, Heinzen was our frequent guest.

He reached New York, after a short stay in England, during the year 1851, and after publishing a newspaper in that city for a few years, he moved to Boston, where he continued its publication with considerable success until the time of his death, about eight years ago.

OSWALD OTTENDORFER.

When Oswald Ottendorfer came to Kaiserslautern in May, 1849, to offer his services to the Provisional Govern-

ment, he wore the uniform of the Academic Legion of the
University of Vienna, where he had been a student, and
where he had taken part in the insurrection of the previous
year, and in the more recent movement in concert with
Kossuth's operations in Hungary. He served during the
ensuing campaign in Southern Germany as volunteer, and
eventually became, like all the rest, an exile in Switzerland,
whence he emigrated to America some time in 1850. We
had known each other in Germany, and when I met him,
shortly after his arrival in New York, during one of my
Sunday vacations from that Long Island cabbage farm,
Ottendorfer was peddling, in utter want and sheer despera-
tion, baskets of gorgeously-labeled beverages of doubtful
composition among houses of questionable resort. When
next I saw him, during the Centennial year, his liveried
coachman drove us from his magnificent office in Printing
House Square to his country-seat opposite the Palisades at
Manhattanville, overlooking the Hudson, where we were
met by his noble wife, whose munificent charitable bequests
will cause her name to be forever remembered in affection-
ate gratitude. We fought our youthful battles over while
enjoying a delightful dinner, and when I congratulated him
upon his remarkable success, I felt that fortune could never
have smiled upon a worthier and more deserving man. His
newspaper, the *New York Staatszeitung*, has an immense
circulation, and is read by the German people without distinction of party; its independent spirit, and the great ability
with which it is edited, form a pleasing contrast with the
prevailing journalism of the day, while the high personal
character of its publisher, and his acknowledged sterling
integrity, are a source of pride to his immediate countrymen; and his genial, tender-hearted kindness is the pleasure
and delight of his numberless friends.

BLENKER.

Blenker appears to have been a soldier of fortune from earliest youth. When a mere boy he served as a volunteer in Greece, during her heroic struggle of deliverance from the yoke of the Turks. During the summer of 1848 he drilled a militia company in the town of Worms, famous for its cathedral and for that memorable trial in which Luther told his judges. "if this is the work of men, it will crumble to pieces of its own accord, but if it is the work of God, it is vain for you to oppose it." And when, in May, 1849. the news reached Blenker of the flight of the Grand Duke of Baden, he promptly marched his militia company up the river to Ludwigshafen and seized the little garrison at the Bavarian end of the bridge, which crosses the Rhine at Mannheim. He was a dashing fellow, sitting well in the saddle, too proud to be anything but brave. He made a bold attempt on one bright Sunday morning to storm the Fortress of Landau, but after receiving a few rounds of grape shot from the ramparts of the fort, he reconsidered his plan and concluded to let Landau alone. He commanded, as well as any one could command such a body, a large force of heterogeneous volunteers, and his energetic, pale-faced little wife rode by his side through all that campaign, from Zweibrucken, on the line between France and Bavaria, through the Palatinate, across the Rhine, down to Mannheim, back to Rastadt and over the shady hills of the Black Forest, past Freiburg, once more across the Rhine into Switzerland.

Just where Blenker spent the short interval between the close of the war of 1849 and his arrival in New York in 1851, I do not now recollect, but well do I remember the dairy farm which he cultivated in Orange County, on the

Hudson, where free buttermilk and aromatic cheese were dispensed in most generous measure to his visiting friends.

He evidently was on hand again promptly in 1861, for we read of his covering the retreat from Bull Run towards Washington. Early in 1862 he commanded a division during the operations of the army in the Shenandoah Valley, but during the latter part of the war his health failed, and he died before its final conclusion.

JOSEPH WEYDEMEYER

was one of those obnoxious Prussian artillery officers whose resignations were demanded somewhere in 1847. In 1848 he was employed on the Cologne-Minden Railroad as engineer, and it was under his tuition that I received the first practical instructions of my profession. After the defeat of the revolutionary movements in 1849, he came to New York, where he engaged in journalistic enterprises, settled subsequently in Milwaukee, and returned to New York in 1860, under an appointment as engineer of the Central Park Commission. In 1861 he enlisted under Fremont, in St. Louis, where at first he took charge of the erection of the fortifications in that vicinity, and afterwards received a lieutenant colonel's commission in the 2d Regiment of Missouri Artillery, in which capacity he spent a long time in Western Missouri fighting the guerrillas and bushwhackers. Towards the close of the war he commanded the 41st Regiment of Missouri Infantry, and was also Commander of the post of St. Louis.

In 1886 he was elected Auditor of St. Louis County, but he had barely entered upon his duties when he died of cholera, in the prime of his life. His wife, who died a few years later in Pittsburgh, was a sister of Dr. Otto Luenig, a distinguished journalist, and publisher of the *New German Gazette*, the leading organ of the Democratic side of Parliament in Frankfurt during the exciting days of 1848 and 1849. Two other brothers, who had taken part in the earlier movement of 1830, and who had taken refuge in Switzerland, were professors in the University of Zurich at the time I enjoyed the hospitality of that delightful city.

LORENZ BRENTANO.

who occupied, during the insurrection of 1849, the position of President of the Provisional Government, and who still lives in Chicago, was born at Mannheim in the Grand Duchy of Baden, in 1813. He received a classical education, studied jurisprudence at Heidelberg and Freiburg, and after graduating practiced law before the Supreme Court of the State. He first distinguished himself as leading counsel for the defence in the celebrated state trial against Gustave von Struve, for high treason. After attaining the legal age he was elected to the Chamber of Deputies, where he soon became the recognized leader of the opposition party.

In 1848 he was elected to Parliament, and after the outbreak in 1849 he became President of the Revolutionary Government, for which he was condemned in contumaciam to imprisonment for life. After his emigration to this country he first settled upon a farm in Kalamazoo County, Michigan; in 1859 he removed to Chicago and commenced the practice of law; in 1862 he served as a member of the Illinois Legislature, and after the expiration of his term he became a member of the Chicago Board of Education.

He was a delegate, in 1868, to the National Republican Convention which nominated Grant and Colfax, and during all this time he was also editor-in-chief and principal proprietor of the *Illinois Staatszeitung.* In 1869 he took advantage of the general amnesty and paid a visit to his native country, from which he returned to recover what was left of his property by the great Chicago fire.

From 1872 to 1876 he served as United States Consul at Dresden, and afterwards was elected to the 45th Congress as a member from the Chicago City District.

I happened to be present in the winter of 1848 at a very amusing and somewhat exciting scene, in which Brentano played a conspicuous part. In the course of a speech, which he delivered on this occasion in Parliament, he alluded in rather disrespectful language to the Crown Prince of Prussia, (the present Emperor,) who had just then returned from his short exile in England, when a young aristocratic member, a nobleman of high rank, took exceptions to Brentano's remarks, and in a greatly excited manner challenged him right there and then for daring to insult the brother of his King. Brentano looked calmly at his assailant, and said in a quiet and dignified tone, "Well, if this little case between the Prince and myself is to be settled by proxy, I will send my coachman to fight you; what time would it suit you to meet him?"

If the bold young aristocrat had been actually kicked by Brentano's coachman, he could not have been more profoundly humiliated.

MAX WEBER,

who had been a Lieutenant in the Army of Baden, and his comrade Schwarz, who parted from his father, when the latter followed the Grand Duke into exile, both performed gallant services in the Union army during the War of the Rebellion. Weber commanded a brigade in General Sedgwick's division of Sumner's 2d Corps at the battles of Fredericksburgh and Antietam, and the bravery of Schwarz's battery of artillery during Grant's operations around Fort Donaldson and Vicksburg is honorably mentioned in the official reports of that campaign.

Besides these few, whose lives I have briefly sketched, there have been and still are hundreds of others, scattered throughout all parts of this Western World, pursuing in modest ways their humble vocations, yet adding, to the best of their ability, their honest shares to its material development and intellectual improvement.

A few years more, and the last exile of '49 will have found refuge in that great asylum where extradition laws are unknown, and where, as I hope, he will not be compelled to serve a probationary term prior to his full admission to citizenship. But his children and his children's children will live on, assimilated, absorbed and Americanized; unmindful of their origin and indifferent to their descent.

The home of my early childhood stands near the border of an inland lake. From its shores rise abruptly a circle of rugged mountain sides, furrowed by ravines and cleft by gorges and valleys, which conduct their tributary streams from the uplands to the basin below. Tumbling in picturesque cascades over precipitous cliffs, rushing in rippling currents over pebbly beds, or flowing smoothly between green, wooded banks, they all mingle at last their liquid contributions with the placid waters of that quiet mountain lake. Often have I watched this charming scene from some commanding point of view, and beheld, with the pleasure of childhood, this ceaseless giving and receiving in the meeting of the waters.

When the sky is clear overhead, its azure tint will be

reflected, with increased intensity, in the mirror-like surface of the water below; and the mingling currents from the affluent streams will barely shade its shore line with a faint and milk-like fringe. But in a storm, when the pouring rain, chased by the raging wind, swells the gentle brooklets into roaring torrents, tearing down and carrying with them whatever obstructs their passage, dissolving the soil which confines them, and scouring the beds over which they flow, then the milky fringe on the shore will change to a rim of deeper dye, darkly outlined along the shore, but growing fainter, as it widens and spreads, and finally melting again by imperceptible degrees into the undisturbed, unchanged and normal tint of the central part of the lake; and upon the outer edge of the agitated waters will at such times float the drift and debris from the mountains around. But a day or two of calm will restore the normal aspect. The froth and foam and the rubbish which came down with the torrent, and which floated conspicuously on its crest and covered the surface of the lake, will disappear with the returning calm; the frothy scum which aimlessly drifted about in circling eddies, will dry and dissolve; the shiny bubbles will burst and the foam evaporate in the rays of the genial sun; the floating rubbish will be cast ashore, and the stranded debris will decay on the beach. But the solid matter, which was held in temporary suspense and solution by the current, will subside in the quiet waters of the lake, and, precipitated upon its bottom, become, in due course of time, part of the everlasting rocks which form its solid and enduring foundation.

It is customary with artists, when they draw historical pictures in which appear groups of famous man, to annex marginal sketches, giving in mere outlines and upon a reduced scale *fac-similes* of the groups in the original, with the names of the persons and other explanatory notes and references.

The picture which I have attempted to draw may require a similar explanation; but all its minor features will become clear in their meaning and application as soon as you recognize in the quiet, pure and placid mountain lake, your own country—America, the country of my adoption.